Praise

"Linda Urick's love of coastal beauty is evident in her poetry, but even more than that, she attempts to draw us into calm contemplation as we reflect upon the powerful resources of the sea."

—Theresa Hickey, Author of *Shy* (2016) and *Resting Place* (2024), Finishing Line Press

# of Salt and Solace

Linda Ripley Urick

Copyright © 2025 by Linda Ripley Urick

All rights reserved. No part of this book may be reproduced in any form or by any electronic or mechanical means, including information storage and retrieval systems, without written permission from the author, except in the case of a reviewer, who may quote brief passages embodied in critical articles or in a review.

Author: Linda Ripley Urick

Book Strategist and Publishing Services: Amy Collette
Cover and Interior Design: Victoria Wolf
Photographer: C. R. Boecklen
Email: ofsaltandsolace@yahoo.com

ISBN: 979-8-218-77502-5

The information contained in this book is for general information and entertainment purposes only. The recommendations, opinions, experiences, observations, or other information contained herein is provided "as is" and neither the author nor publisher make any representations or warranties of any kind, express or implied, about the accuracy, suitability, reliability or completeness of this book's content. All recommendations are made without guarantee on the part of the author and publisher. To the maximum extent permitted by law, the author and publisher disclaim all liability from this publication's use. In no event will either author or publisher be liable to any reader for any loss or damage whatsoever arising from the use of the information contained in this book.

Contents

In Memory ix
Introduction 1
Alpha 4
Shore Leave 6
For the Love of Him 8
Time Holds Its Breath 10
Captain Captain SOS 12
Wondrous Moments 14
Sunday at the Beach 16
Adieu Adieu 18
On Piper's Wing 20
Yonder Yacht 22
Bird Lady Rules of Gold 24
Terrapin CSI 26
Sea Turtle Legacy 28
"Hearts and Elbows" Origin 32
Hearts and Elbows 34
Birthing Babes 36
Shhhhh……..Turtle Sleeping 38
Solace 40
Glorious Morning 42

Cheep Divorce	44
Pregnant Sea Oats	46
Misty Morning	48
Hearts and Towels	50
Beach Bells	52
Honeymoon	56
Priceless	58
Majestic Sunset	60
Kingdom Chaos	62
After the Storm	64
On Willet's Wing	66
Shore Delivery	68
Hearts at Sea	70
Sun Daze	72
All My Cares Away	74
Seashore Calling	76
Twilight	78
Omega	80
Acknowledgments	83
About the Author	85
Thank You	87

In Memory

Of Salt and Solace is dedicated posthumously to Currie George Harbour, my soul mate. But for his encouragement and "nagging," this book would not have been written.

We were two independent individuals who chose to spend a life together. We were both beach lovers. He loved to fish and built his successful business, Sea Harbour, around fly-fishing clothing. I loved to write. We wrote and fished our way from Boca Grande, Florida, to Bermuda to Ireland.

Our journey of 36 memorable years became a patchwork quilt of experiences. I would write a poem for each of life's passages–birthdays, graduations, passings and special occasions. With each poem, Currie would say "Linda, you have a gift and you need to share it." I was always too busy with children, work, and everyday responsibilities to do it.

It is only after his passing, I have the time to honor the confidence he gifted me.

Of Salt and Solace is for Currie and all the wonderful memories we made at the shore.

Introduction

World weary, I come to the shore. The beach is actually a place to gain perspective, to replenish, to recharge — to fill the chalice of the soul.

Daybreak takes a misty breath. The surf is still — a foggy mirror begging to be wiped clean with sunshine. At times, I too am a foggy mirror searching for light. I lose my center. Like the tide, the shore pulls me back, calms my weary soul and gives me hope. Its vastness speaks to me of life's possibilities. Its salt heals my wounds. Its constant movement mimics the ebb and flow of life.

My thirsty soul drinks

This book is about the power of the shore in my life. How a visit to the gentle, rolling water can pull me from a dusty side road back onto life's highway. How the salty air can fuel my spirit and boost it into life's orbit. How the beauty of the vast open water prepares my soul for the marathon of life.

It is my wish to share my joyful visits to the shore. To this day the sea is my source of strength – my center. Through this book, it is my hope that you too will be able to tap into the mystical power of the shore and fill the chalice of your soul.

The waves echo behind me.
Patience – Faith – Openness,
Is what the sea has to teach.

Anne Morrow Lindbergh
Gift from the Sea

Alpha

There is a yellow cottage
    Beside the deep blue sea
        A tiny yellow cottage
            It waits there just for me

Windows lush with flowers
    Ivy climbs the stair
        Sand upon the doorstep
            Orchids in the air

Seashells grace the counter
    Dollars made of sand
        Fragrance of the tropics
            Egrets close at hand

Soft caressing breezes
    Easy chair nearby
        Listen to the ocean
            Behold the azure sky

Complete with trusted journal
    A lovely cup of tea
        'Tis my own sweet Heaven
            Beside the deep blue sea

Shore Leave

Lo the shore is calling
    Curly crinoline surf
        Lo the shore is calling
           I must get back to work

Lo the shore is calling
    Royal pelican squadron
        Lo the shore is calling
           I must beg your pardon

Lo the shore is calling
    Brisk Bahama breeze
        Lo the shore is calling
           No - clients I must please

Lo the shore is calling
    Frangipani air
        Lo the shore is calling
           Delinquency beware

Lo the shore is calling
    Brilliant sultry sunset
        Lo the shore is calling
           Obligations must be kept

Lo the shore is calling
    Hear its lovely roar
        Lo the shore is calling
           Take Me
                To the shore

For the Love of Him

Shivering with goose bumps
This sight in front of me
Magnificent, majestic
My love – the open sea

His eyes behold my presence
And blink back glistening tears
Still moved by my arrival
After all these years

Wafts of musk and ancient worlds
Beckon me to stay
At his side forever
With cares so far away

His sea mist wraps around me
Holds me close and still
Quiets pulsing heart
Bends me to his will

Here I'll stay a thousand years
And not just on a whim
Here to stay a thousand years
For the love of him

Time Holds Its Breath

Silken mist rests like a
    Kimono over sleepy sea
        Hides its swells and curves

Tumultuous tide runs out
    Greets lonely foghorn
        Sea gulls call to sleepy sun
            Awake

Conchs in sand beds
    Lay exposed
        Await adventures
            Atop mahogany desks

Wave's military cadence
    Releases battalions of foam
        Palapas stand at attention
            Frangipani languishes

Sea mist thickens
    Blurs the line
        'Twixt sea and sand
            Surf's drumbeat rumbles

Distant palms cluster
    Lose their individuality
        To the foggy fraternity

Sea oats still and straight
    Await whispers of wind
        Time holds its breath

Captain Captain
SOS

Captain Captain
SOS
Rescue sailboat
In distress

Sailboat anchored
Right offshore
Twists and turns
Against the moor

Writhes and wriggles
To be free
Tethered torment
On the sea

Once bilious sails
Do sulk and pout
Yawn and yearn
To come about

Boastful boom
Secured and bound
Does like the eerie
Pendulum pound

Sea breeze whispers
Fore and aft
Who is here
To man this craft

Captain Captain
SOS
Rescue sailboat
In distress

Wondrous Moments

Let me be the first one
To show my child the sea
Let me be the first one
And happy I will be

    Step upon the virgin beach
    Carved and shaped by time
    Use our toes as shovels
    In sugar sand so fine

        Chase the flocks of shore birds
        Swift and loud and free
        Go and try to catch one
        Bring him back to me

            The wonder of the seashell
            An ocean – can you hear
            Listen to the seashell
            Hear it loud and clear

                Step into the water
                Warm waves will kiss your feet
                Step into the water
                Foam circles toes do meet

                    Bring to me your treasures
                    In my hand to stay
                    Saved for all my children
                    Memories of this day

                        Let me be the first one
                        To show my child the sea
                        Let me be the first one
                        And happy I will be

Sunday at the Beach

Kaleidoscope
Umbrellas
Dance

Jasmine fingers
Waft
Linger

Bikini Babes
Bask
Shimmer

Solitary swimmer
Floats
Suspended

Pelican battalions
Halt
Maneuver

Daring dolphin
Delights
Disappears

Graceful gulls
Gather
Giggle

Slanted sails
Shadow
Sultry sunset

Adieu Adieu

Sandy piper
> By the sea
> Pause a bit
> And chat with me

> Busy busy
>> All the day
>> Have you no time
>> To stop and play

>> Watch I do
>>> Your fuzzy frame
>>> Armed with spirit
>>> Not to tame

>>> Chase the waves
>>>> Out from shore
>>>> Hurry back
>>>> Chase some more

>>>> Cherub children
>>>>> Reach for you
>>>>> Off you go
>>>>> Adieu adieu

>>>>> Skitter skitter
>>>>>> Everywhere
>>>>>> Not a moment
>>>>>> Us to spare

>>>>>> Finally
>>>>>>> I am resigned
>>>>>>> Chat you won't
>>>>>>> You have no time

On Piper's Wing

"When my life is filled with salt, I seek the solace of the sea."

Sandpipers skitter across the wasteland of my soul
I catch a ride on tiny wing
Soft warm breezes brush my face
Loosen my hair
Launch my spirit

    We cruise a foamy shoreline
    Pregnant with shells from the twilight tide
    Sunlight massages an aching mind
    As we soar out o'er open water

        Ghostly schools of silver fish
        Yawn in the morning light
        A lone gull screeches his blessing
        Brisk jasmine air fills my lungs

            Coral reefs take shape 'neath dancing waves
            Baby dolphin leaps sends beach bunnies to water's edge
            Sleek and shiny he frolics and flirts
            Passing pelican turns for home with morning's catch

                Sea oats wave a greeting as we touch warm sand
                Sandpiper tracks give birth to
                Sprigs of grass and flower beds
                In the wasteland of my soul

Yonder Yacht

Yonder yacht is anchored
Gleaming just off shore
Long and low and sultry
Fifty feet or more

Where and whence could it have come
Why appear just now
Might they be awake
Or sleeping in the bow

Will they cook their breakfast
And serve it on top deck
Or will they place an order
Perhaps eggs benedict

Will they pull the anchor
And sail to glamorous place
Perhaps to meet discreetly
Reclusive famous face

I wish them well their journey
Lots of happiness too
Perhaps on your next visit
I shall sail with you

Bird Lady Rules of Gold

There is a lady
    On the beach
        Birds do follow
            For their treats

She talks to them
    They understand
        Do not fear
           Her giving hand

She watches o'er
    Her feathered flock
        They too watch
           From jetty rock

See her rescue
    Just in time
        Shore bird caught
           In fishing line

Tucks him secure
    Beneath her arm
        Shuttles him
           Away from harm

She helps us
    To understand
        How to treat
           Our fellow man

Terrapin CSI

Yellow crime tape
'Tween lounge chairs
Yellow crime tape
Do beware

Yellow crime tape
On the beach
Yellow crime tape
Not to breach

What could cause
This creepy sight
For all to see
In Paradise

From wave to sand
Trace the tracks
Sea to shore
And then back

Suspicious now
I look around
Spot the sign
Above the ground

Do not touch
Our turtle's nest
Please protect
Let them rest

Dim the lights
Quiet please
Birth of babes
Soon to be

Sea Turtle Legacy

In dark of night
To shore she creeps
Great with child
She cannot sleep

Three hundred pounds
Is hers to carry
Slowly surely
Not to tarry

Lumbers on
Through deeper sand
Searches for
A higher stand

At last she finds
The perfect site
Fiery flash
Cell phone light

Round about
In slow motion
Back to safety
Of the ocean

Buoyed by
The salty sea
Swims up shore
Light to flee

Once again
She does climb
To select
Spot sublime

Flippers struggle
Lift her shell
Mark the sand
Secrets tell

All the night
She digs and labors
Makes a home
For her babies

Exhausted now
She takes her leave
Just reward
Her Legacy

"Hearts and Elbows" Origin

At sunrise, I stroll along a pristine stretch of beach and come upon a popular sunset bar quiet and deserted in the morning light.

The murmur of a soft surf, the effortless glide of a lone egret and the wafts of night jasmine fill the air.

What? The beach entrance to the ever-crowded nightly cocktail scene is flagged in yellow "Beware" tape!

Last night, a sea turtle had chosen that very spot to build her nest and deposit her eggs. Convenient for her, not so for the bar and hotel attached to her nest.

To the bar owner's surprise, the patrons adopted the nest, toasted it nightly, bet on the date and time of birth, and proceeded to protect it from all harm.

The birth of the baby turtles caused great celebration and even more toasts.

"Hearts and Elbows" is a salute to the wisdom of the mama sea turtle.

Hearts and Elbows

Folks do travel near and far
To toast the day at "Sunset Bar"
Not at all to be left out
Mama turtle comes about

In black of night she makes her nest
In full view of elbow's rest
Why oh why was she inclined
To choose this spot for nesting time

Yellow tape does mark the scene
None can pass in between
Reroute the entrance to the bar
Detour to the door afar

Stop the traffic dim the lights
Babies sleeping out of sight
Lots of tourists stop and wait
Guard the nest and speculate

Bets are made
On baby numbers
While still watching
Turtle slumber

Suddenly the sand does quake
Quiet shhhh no sound to make
Tiny turtles one then three
Scurry to the moonlit sea

Mama turtle
Is so smart
As elbows bend
So goes the heart

Birthing Babes

Moonlight
    Mirror
        Glints

Damp
    Sand
        Cracks

Fissures
    Form

Sandy
    Womb
        Writhes

Tiny
    Turtles
        Breach

Flippers
    Fly

Salty
    Ocean
        Opens

Safe
    Harbor
        Secured

Shhhhh……..
Turtle Sleeping

Hear ye Hear ye
    Nesting time
        Dim the lights
            Or get a fine

Tiptoe Tiptoe
    Quiet keep
        Tiny turtles
            Fast asleep

Then one starry
    Moonlit night
        Mini turtles
            Chart their flight

Little bodies
    Born to roam
        Embrace the ocean
            Journey home

Solace

   Tired toes
      Sink in wet sand
         Warm waves whisper
            Shiny shells dance
               Drowsy daybreak yawns
                  Balmy breeze brushes
                     Pallid skin plumps

      Tiny sailboat skims
         Silver wake streams
            Jaunty jasmine wafts
               Florid fragrance lingers
                  Weary mind wonders
                  Salty solace

Glorious Morning

Oh what a glorious morning
Has been gifted me
Oh what a glorious morning
In my cottage by the sea

    Waves caress the shoreline
    Creating eyelet hems
    Waves caress the shoreline
    Their welcome to extend

        Shore birds chirp and chatter
        As if to say "Hello"
        Shore birds chirp and chatter
        Cheeky chicks in tow

            The snowy egret fishes
            Oblivious to me
            The snowy egret fishes
            Regal strong and free

                Morning's pregnant mist
                Gentle humid fingers
                Morning's pregnant mist
                Circles swirls and lingers

                    Oh what a glorious morning
                    In my cottage by the sea
                    Oh what a glorious morning
                    Has been gifted me

Cheep Divorce

Two cheeps on a sea oat
    Looking back at me
        Two cheeps on a sea oat
            Chipper as can be

Perched atop a tiny stalk
    Swaying with each gust
        Chirp and chat for hours
            Dawn 'til nearly dusk

Two cheeps on a sea oat
    Bend it to the ground
        He soars off and she is left
            Bounces up and down

One cheep on a sea oat
    Single and carefree
        One cheep on a sea oat
            Winks her eye at me

Pregnant Sea Oats

In morning's sultry air
    Sea oat fronds
        Heavy burdens bear
            Bend in twilight mist

Expectant with seeds
    Bow with the weight
        Day's beginning
            Anxiously await

Sunlight touches laden tips
    All the seeds to hold
        Brilliant transformation
            Harvest turns to gold

Sea oat fronds
    In morning's sultry air
        Dressed in ingots
            Laden there

Misty Morning

It is a misty morning
With absence of the sun
Sea and sky together
Consummate as one

        Lazy sleepy dolphins
        Roll and wave at me
        On this foggy morning
        Beside the peaceful sea

                Waves come in more slowly
                To greet the sleepy shore
                Wake up and turn the shells
                Gorgeous day in store

Pelicans on maneuvers
Up and down the beach
Search for tasty breakfast
In waters out of reach

        The lonely foghorn bellows
        Announces morning light
        The sea mist lifts her skirts
        To the sun's delight

                Shore birds join together
                To orchestrate a song
                Whose melody continues
                All the bright day long

                        Sea and sky do separate
                        In the light of day
                        Sea and sky do separate
                        Go their separate ways

Hearts and Towels

Lonely blue striped towel
    On morning beach alone
        Wet abandoned lifeless
            Owner name unknown

Adjacent lies a perfect heart
    Initials in the sand
        Carved by star crossed lovers
            In nocturnal hand

Were they kids or newlyweds
    Or old loves just like us
        Where are they this morning
            Having spent their lust

Here's to them where e'er they are
    Twin hearts forever be
        Carved in stars so high above
            Beside the rolling sea

Beach Bells

Wedding at the Beach Club
Excitement reigns supreme
Wedding at the Beach Club
Every couple's dream

Velvet lawns are preened and cut
Every blade erect
Velvet lawns are preened and cut
Perfection to expect

Palms appear from nowhere
Just to frame the sea
Palms appear from nowhere
Wedding vows to be

Arch of angel's wings
Completes the blessed scene
Awaits the loving words
Of two who dare to dream

Music from the shorebirds
And the rolling sea
Will be duly summoned
Provide the melody

Snowy egret usher
In his coat of white
Welcomes guests aplenty
Just before twilight

As skies turn to magenta
Wedding march begins
Sunset orchestrated
Heaven's diadem

Bride a starry vision
In her gown of white
Joins her handsome partner
At Angel's Arch tonight

With love the vows recited
In front of every guest
Promising the future
For this couple blessed

Every star in Heaven
Appears as if to say
God speed to these two lovers
On their wedding day

Honeymoon

Saucer moon
Upon the sea
Sailboat anchor
You and me

Lacquered water
Near and far
Brilliant mirror
Shooting star

Time and hearts
Stopped and still
Tomorrow's cares
Small and nil

Toast and promise
Candlelight
Touch caress
Velvet night

Gentle rocking
Down below
Womb of water
Serene souls

Priceless

Lonely sailboat
    Out to sea
        Tack on in
            Rescue me

Chart a course
    Upon a star
        Take my soul
            Journey far

        Let the waves
            Lull me to sleep
                Capture me
                    My mind to keep

            Bring the breeze
                Blow cares away
                    Stress relief
                        With each sway

              Hear the gull
                'Tis my alarm
                    Daybreak sunny
                        Soft and warm

                Catch a fish
                    Throw him back
                      Catch another
                        Maybe "jack"

                Daydream moment
                    To entice
                      Perfect pleasure
                        Without price

Majestic Sunset

Ethereal evening majesty
Over yonder bay
Ethereal evening majesty
Glorious display

Pink of pink rose of rose
Birthing clouds portray
Pink of pink rose of rose
Herald the close of day

Celestial bilious giants
Roam the sky tonight
Celestial bilious giants
Battle sunset light

Giant flaming embers
Reflect on salty stage
Giant flaming embers
Breathless brilliant rage

Sky and sea and all the earth
Ablaze at even tide
Sky and sea and all the earth
Still to Heaven's might

Ethereal evening majesty
Glorious display
Ethereal evening majesty
Over yonder bay

Kingdom Chaos

Dragonflies
    Do congregate
        Portend the storm
            Levitate

Palm frond missiles
    Pound the ground
        Coconuts
            Float in mounds

Churning water
    Once was blue
        Now dirty grey
            Purpose skewed

Ravenous clouds
    Full of strife
        Bellow thunder
            Rowdy rife

Sunshine runs
    No place to hide
        Sand succumbs
            To rising tide

Skies turn eerie
    Peptic yellow
        Regurgitate
            On shore so mellow

Angry waves
    Race inland
        Bound to conquer
            Beast and man   Kingdom chaos
                                        It does reign
                                            Powered by
                                                  A hurricane

After the Storm

Monet mist
    Blankets
        Morning sun

Curious dolphin
    Surfaces
        Chases night

Breeze fingers
    Nudge
        Sleepy water

Pelican patrols
    Glide
        Await breakfast

Minnow schools
    Glisten
        Maneuver close

Gentle waves
    Caress
        Sandy beach

Persistent sunlight
    Awakens
        Drowsy day

    Mona Lisa morning

On Willet's Wing

On willet's wing
    I shall fly
        Strut my stripes
            'Neath the sky

Soar out o'er
    The ocean blue
        Catch a thermal
            Maybe two

Drop each care
    Upon the sea
        Watch it float
            Away from me

Journey back to
    Shells and sand
        Burden lifted
            Life in hand

Shore Delivery

Giant swells
Spew
Misty contractions

Groans from ocean's floor
Announce
Laboring rollers

Sea gulls
Circle
Scream

Pipers
Take wing
Scatter

Waves and shore
Explode
Give birth

Watery eyelet petticoats
Embrace
Grateful shorelines

Hushed voices
Witness
Shore's delivery

Hearts at Sea

Give to me the seashore
I'll build on it a home
Give to me the seashore
And I shall never roam

Give me an umbrella
Two chairs striped in blue
Sit beside the ocean
Just a while with you

Inhale the far horizon
Drink in the peaceful view
Listen to the sea gulls
Chatting out of tune

Feel the air caress us
Warm sun on our backs
Feel the air caress us
Nothing does this lack

Yes there's nothing better
Nothing more we need
Than sitting near the ocean
It is sublime indeed

Sun Daze

Rising sun
Whispering breeze

Virgin sand
Stately palms

Busy pipers
Eyelet shoreline

Setting sun
Magenta sky

Mirrored water
Pregnant moon

Diamond planets
Stardust sea

Gently touch
Velvet night

All My Cares Away

Ray of morning sun
    Touches skin of night
        Ray of morning sun
            Opens eye lids tight

  Warmth of its persistence
      Nudges me awake
          Warmth of its persistence
              Gently dreams do take

        Yes the shoreline calls me
            Oft it speaks my name
              Yes the shoreline calls me
                  All my thoughts to tame

          Soft breezes touch my shoulders
              Shimmer down my arms
                  Soft breezes touch my shoulders
                      Distance from all harm

            Placid water twinkles
              Just a hint of breeze
                  Placid water twinkles
                      Sets my mind at ease

            Puffy clouds do frame the sea
              And are reflected there
                  Puffy clouds do frame the sea
                  A masterpiece so rare

            My soul descends to quiet
              All my cares away
                  My soul descends to quiet
                      On this brilliant day

Seashore Calling

Take a single seashell
And make it all your own
Take it in your suitcase
Wherever you may roam

Listen to the ocean
In Greece or London town
Place it on your nightstand
As you journey round

You won't forget the seashore
And its magnificence
You won't forget the seashore
When ancient world's entrance

For the memories embedded

In every shell you find

Will call you to the seashore

Each and every time

Twilight

Give me the shore at twilight
    Whilst mist is on the moor

Give me the shore at twilight
    Shadowed figures to explore

Give me the shore at twilight
    Where velvet waves entwine

Give me the shore at twilight
    Cool sculptured sand divine

Give me the shore at twilight
    When sunset blazes red

Give me the shore at twilight
    With nightfall straight ahead

Give me the shore at twilight
    Whilst mist is on the moor

Omega

Choose Dear Lord a special place
The perfect end for me
Put me in my cottage
Beside the open sea

Make for me the coffee
And a roaring fire
Hand to me a book
And then I shall retire

Quietly and softly
You can call my name
Right here by the ocean
No fanfare crowds or fame

We shall hold a lovely discourse
On only things that matter
In silence you to follow
Up the golden ladder

There to greet my mother
Whom I have missed so much
Standing in her apron
Arms waiting for my touch

Choose Dear Lord this special place
A perfect end for me
Put me in my cottage
Beside the open sea

Acknowledgments

To Krissy for her "flash drive" expertise.

To Heather for setting a "publishing" example.

To Amy for her guidance and encouragement to get this book into print.

About the Author

Born and raised on a Midwest farm, Linda discovered early on she was not cut out for a career in farming. In attempting to gas up the tractor, she put the gas in the radiator, causing mayhem during the harvest season.

On a family trip to Lido Beach, Florida, she fell in love at first sight. She had "sand in her shoes" and orchestrated her return after college graduation. Her borrowed 1957 overhauled Chevy used 25 quarts of oil on the 1700-mile trip to Miami.

IBM in Miami became her home for the next several years as Linda worked as an Educational Services Representative, followed by marriage and children.

Eventually, wealth management and the financial industry became a 20-year passion and career. Concurrently, Linda enrolled in a writing class, visited the beach every Saturday, and penned her shore excursions into a book of poetry.

She currently resides in Colorado near her daughter and son-in-law, and loves reading, charity work, and traveling back to the beach.

Linda can be reached by email at *ofsaltandsolace@yahoo.com*.

Thank you

Thank you for reading *Of Salt and Solace*.

If you enjoyed the experience, please consider leaving a review on Amazon.

(Search *Of Salt and Solace* **and click on the Stars/Review area)**

Please be specific about what touched you, or what you will remember most.

This will help other readers know that *Of Salt and Solace* might be for them as well.

With gratitude,
Linda Ripley Urick

www.ingramcontent.com/pod-product-compliance
Lightning Source LLC
Chambersburg PA
CBHW030241010526
44107CB00030B/1298/J